HERBAL REMEDIES
FOR INSOMNIA

Discover The Power Of Nature's Healing
Through Herbs For Embracing Key
Practices For Restful Nights, Holistic
Wellness And Transforming Your Sleep
Routine

DR. CARDEN KYRIE

DISCLAIMER

The only goal of this book is informational. Every effort has been taken by the author and publisher to ensure that the information provided is accurate. But the material in this book is given "as is," without any express or implied representation, warranty, or condition as to its accuracy, completeness, or suitability for any particular purpose.

Any loss, damage, or injury resulting from using the information in this book, or from any action or decision made as a result of such use, will not be covered by the author's or publisher's liability. It is recommended that readers seek the assistance of a certified specialist for guidance specific to their situation.

The opinions and viewpoints conveyed in this book belong to the author and may not necessarily represent the official stance or policies of any specified organizations or people. Any likeness to real-life occurrences, places, or people—living or deceased—is wholly coincidental.

No specific product, service, or therapy discussed in this book is endorsed by the author or publisher. Any reference to goods or services is made only for informative reasons and is not intended as a recommendation or endorsement.

Before making any judgments or acting on any information, readers are urged to independently confirm it all. Any unfavorable effects or repercussions arising from the usage of the material included in this book are disclaimed by the author and publisher.

By using this book, you consent to absolving the publisher and author of any and all claims, obligations, or losses resulting from your use of the material in it.

I appreciate your cooperation and understanding.

TABLE OF CONTENTS

CHAPTER ONE

INTRODUCTION TO INSOMNIA

WHY USE HERBAL INSOMNIA REMEDIES?

Herbal therapies for insomnia have attracted a lot of interest and attention in the field of complementary and alternative medicine. A significant percentage of people worldwide suffer from insomnia, a common sleep problem marked by trouble sleeping or staying asleep. Herbal cures are popular because people are drawn to all-natural, non-invasive therapies that align with a holistic view of the human body and its relationship to the natural world.

The uses of herbal treatments for insomnia stems from the idea that some plants have healing qualities that can ease stress, encourage relaxation, and help people fall asleep. This method is in line with age-old medical procedures that have been handed down through the generations, which use the therapeutic qualities of herbs to treat a range of illnesses, including sleep difficulties.

Proponents contend that in addition to treating the symptoms, herbal therapies work to bring the body's natural processes back into balance, leading to a more long-lasting and sustainable cure for insomnia.

THE HEALTH EFFECTS OF INSOMNIA

It is impossible to overestimate the effects of insomnia on health because they go beyond simple sleep deprivation. Many health problems have been linked to chronic insomnia, including mood disorders, cognitive decline, and a higher risk of cardiovascular disease. There is a complex relationship between sleep and general health, and sleep cycle disturbances can have a domino effect on both physiological and psychological issues. Consequently, investigating herbal treatments for insomnia becomes an endeavor to improve general well-being in addition to improving sleep quality.

RECOGNIZING THE FUNCTION OF SLEEP IN GENERAL WELL-BEING

It is essential to comprehend how important sleep is to general health to recognize how important treating insomnia is. Sleep is an essential part of the body's healing processes and is crucial for mental clarity, emotional stability, and physical well-being. The body heals and rebuilds itself, solidifies memories, and controls several physiological processes while we sleep. These vital functions are disturbed by inadequate or poor-quality sleep, which leads to a host of health problems.

Sleep has an impact on mental and emotional aspects of well-being, including mood, stress levels, and the capacity to handle obstacles in life. In this framework, herbal medicines for insomnia are seen as tools that support overall health and vitality in addition to improving sleep quality. The interdependence of many facets of health is highlighted by this holistic viewpoint, which highlights the significance of taking the full person into account when looking for sleep disorder remedies.

Research into herbal sleep aids is indicative of a larger movement in favor of holistic approaches to health and wellness. It recognizes the complex relationship that exists between the natural world and the human body and looks for remedies that support the individual's balance and harmony in addition to relieving symptoms. The deep effects of insomnia on health highlight how urgent it is to treat sleep disorders as essential components of total well-being rather than just isolated issues.

CHAPTER TWO

INSOMNIA OVERVIEW

THE MEANING AND KINDS OF SLEEPLESSNESS

Despite having the chance to sleep, people with insomnia have trouble falling asleep, remaining asleep, or getting restorative sleep. It is a widespread problem that has the potential to seriously affect a person's general health and quality of life. There are various forms of insomnia, and each has unique difficulties.

Short-term acute sleeplessness is frequently brought on by stress or a particular event. It usually goes away on its own without the need for medical attention and can linger for a few days to a few weeks. On the other side, chronic insomnia lasts longer, typically for three months or longer and at least three nights a week. This type of sleeplessness could be linked to long-term pressures, mental health issues, or underlying medical diseases.

Periodically occurring, transient insomnia is frequently associated with alterations in sleep habits or external circumstances. For example, temporary sleeplessness may be exacerbated by shift work, jet lag, or an abrupt change in daily schedule. While secondary insomnia results from other health conditions like depression, anxiety, or chronic pain, primary insomnia is a distinct problem that does not manifest as a symptom of any other medical condition.

TYPICAL CAUSES AND INITIATORS

Effective insomnia management requires an understanding of the causes and triggers of the condition. Psychological elements like stress, worry, or sadness may be common reasons. Insomnia can also be influenced by environmental variables, such as loud noises or uncomfortable sleeping environments. The issue may be made worse by specific drugs, lifestyle decisions like drinking or using coffee, and underlying medical disorders like restless legs syndrome or sleep apnea.

THE SIGNIFICANCE OF DETERMINING FUNDAMENTAL PROBLEMS

Since treating the underlying cause of insomnia can sometimes be more successful than treating the symptoms alone, it is crucial to uncover any underlying problems. To address the psychological and environmental variables causing insomnia, lifestyle adjustments, stress management strategies, and cognitive-behavioral therapy are frequently advised. If a medical issue is found to be the cause of the insomnia, addressing the illness may help.

It's also critical to comprehend the link between mental health and insomnia. Both mental health illnesses and chronic insomnia have a reciprocal relationship that can lead to the onset or worsening of mental health diseases. This reciprocal link emphasizes the necessity of a thorough strategy to address sleep-related problems as well as underlying psychological causes.

Insomnia is a complex sleep condition with a range of manifestations and possible causes. Understanding the various elements that might lead to sleep disruptions and the difference between acute and chronic insomnia is vital. Determining the underlying reasons for insomnia is essential to creating efficient treatment plans, enhancing the general quality of sleep, and enhancing mental health. Resolving underlying problems—medical, psychological, or environmental—is essential to providing long-term relief from insomnia and encouraging a regular sleep schedule.

CHAPTER THREE

OVERVIEW OF HERBAL REMEDIES

HISTORICAL VIEWS OF COMPLEMENTARY MEDICINE

Botanical medicine, sometimes referred to as phytotherapy or herbal medicine, has a long and varied history spanning numerous cultures. Herbs have been used medicinally since ancient times when shamans and traditional healers used the power of plants to cure a wide range of illnesses. Herbal treatments, for instance, were an essential component of traditional Chinese medicine in ancient China, where practitioners trusted in the harmony of yin and yang and the balance of qi.

Similar to this, India's traditional Ayurvedic medicine uses a wide variety of herbs as part of its all-encompassing approach to healing. Along with the Romans, the Greeks and Romans also made important contributions to herbal therapy. Hippocrates, for example, emphasized the value of utilizing nature's abundance for healing. Monastic societies in Europe conserved and developed herbal knowledge during the Middle Ages by growing medicinal gardens and compiling comprehensive herbals.

BENEFITS AND THINGS TO THINK ABOUT FOR HERBAL REMEDIES

The natural source of herbal remedies many of which are derived straight from plants or plant extracts is one of their main benefits. Those looking for holistic and alternative methods to wellness find this innate connection to nature intriguing. When opposed to certain synthetic pharmaceuticals, herbal therapies are frequently thought to be kinder to the body and have fewer negative effects. Furthermore, a lot of herbs have a wide range of bioactive components that can target different parts of an illness, offering a comprehensive and multidimensional approach to treatment.

But before experimenting with herbal medicines, it's important to recognize several important factors. Inconsistent outcomes may arise from the variations in the content of herbal medicines caused by elements like as growing techniques and soil characteristics. Herbal product standardization becomes difficult, and herbal remedies can differ in potency from batch to batch. Furthermore, since certain herbs may alter how drugs are metabolized, interactions between conventional pharmaceuticals and herbs should be carefully explored.

INCLUDING HERBS IN A HOLISTIC WELLNESS APPROACH

The premise that health is a complex interaction of physical, mental, and emotional components is aligned with the incorporation of herbs into a holistic approach to wellness. Herbal treatments address the fundamental imbalances in the body as well as the symptoms, which is how they complement holistic approaches. By highlighting the connections between many facets of a person's health, holistic healthcare encourages preventative rather than reactive approaches to disease management.

Herbal medicines can be integrated with other wellness techniques like exercise, mindfulness, and diet in a holistic paradigm to provide a thorough and individualized treatment plan. This integrative method takes into account each person's particular lifestyle, constitution, and surroundings. Herbalists and holistic health professionals frequently work with people to educate them about self-care, promoting a better awareness of their bodies and a feeling of accountability for their well-being.

The historical background of herbal therapy, along with the benefits and issues surrounding herbal medicines, emphasize how critical it is to incorporate herbs into a comprehensive strategy for overall wellness. Acknowledging the interdependence of mental, emotional, and physical health, people can set out on a path to holistic health by utilizing other components of a holistic lifestyle together with the healing properties of the natural world.

CHAPTER FOUR

HERBS THAT HELP YOU UNWIND AND CALM

THE NATURAL CALMING HERB, CHAMOMILE

For generations, people have praised chamomile, also known as "nature's calming agent," for its ability to induce relaxation. Originating from Asteraceae flowers, chamomile is well known for its calming and stress-relieving properties. Apigenin, one of the plant's constituents, interacts with receptors in the brain to produce a calming effect.

Tea made from chamomile is a popular way for people to take advantage of its calming effects. This age-old cure is beloved for its mild taste as well as its relaxing properties, which make it a well-liked option for de-stressing before bed or handling stress during the day.

VALERIAN ROOT: AN OLD FASHIONED SLEEPING PILL

With historical roots in ancient Greece and Rome, valerian root has shown to be a reliable traditional sleep aid over time. A perennial herb found in many parts of the world, valerian grows everywhere. Chemicals like valerenic acid, which have a calming impact on the neurological system, are found in its roots. Because of this, valerian is a useful treatment for fostering calm and enhancing the quality of sleep. Although its precise mode of action is yet unknown, valerian is thought to increase the brain's synthesis of GABA, a neurotransmitter that controls nerve impulses. Valerian root is still a well-liked option for people looking for a natural way to treat sleep difficulties because it is frequently taken as a supplement or in tea form.

PASSIONFLOWER: CALMING STRESS AND ENCOURAGING REST

The flower passionflower, which is renowned for its vivid and detailed petals, has long been used to reduce anxiety and encourage sound sleep. The plant's anxiolytic (anxiety-reducing) and sedative properties are attributed to substances like flavonoids and alkaloids. Similar to the effects of several prescription anxiety drugs, passionflower is thought to raise GABA levels in the brain. People can choose the most convenient manner for them by selecting from a variety of forms of this botanical treatment, such as teas, tinctures, and supplements. Because of its gentle yet potent properties, passionflower is a useful tool for stress relief and calming down.

LEMON BALM: A MILD ANESTHETIC

As a member of the mint family, lemon balm is known for having mild sedative qualities that reduce stress and promote calm. The herb's anxiolytic properties are attributed to its constituents, including flavonoids and rosmarinic acid. Lemon balm is frequently used to treat anxiety, tension, and sleep disturbances. Lemon balm, whether ingested as a tea or as a supplement, is prized for its subtle flavor and easy incorporation into everyday activities. It demonstrates the potential to enhance mood and cognitive function in addition to its ability to reduce stress. Lemon balm has a long history of being used as a calming herb, which makes it a popular option for anyone looking for a mild and natural way to unwind.

CHAPTER FIVE

ADAPTOGENIC PLANTS TO REDUCE STRESS

ASHWAGANDHA: HARMONIZING MIND AND BODY

The adaptogenic herb ashwagandha, which has its roots in Ayurvedic medicine, has drawn a lot of interest due to its ability to reduce stress. Ashwagandha, sometimes known as "Indian Ginseng," is well known for its capacity to promote mental and physical equilibrium. Because of the herb's adaptogenic properties, it aids in the body's ability to adjust to stimuli and maintain equilibrium. It is thought that ashwagandha influences the synthesis of cortisol, a hormone linked to the stress response, therefore modifying the body's reaction to stress. In doing so, it might lessen stress and anxiety symptoms, promoting serenity and general wellbeing. Furthermore, ashwagandha is well-known for its neuroprotective qualities, which support mental clarity and cognitive function.

It is an important ally in improving holistic well-being because of its all-encompassing approach to stress management.

RHODIOLA ROSEA: EASING FATIGUE AND STRESS

Another powerful adaptogen that has long been used in traditional medicine is Rhodiola Rosea, especially in cold climates like Siberia. Rhodiola Rosea, often known as the "arctic root" or "golden root," is well known for its capacity to fend off exhaustion and stress. The body may adjust to a variety of stimuli, including mental and physical stress, thanks to the adaptogenic qualities of the plant. It is thought that rhodiola increases the body's resistance by assisting the adrenal glands and controlling the release of stress hormones. This adaptogen is well-known for increasing energy levels and enhancing both mental and physical endurance. Rhodiola Rosea plays an important function in promoting vitality and general resilience in the face of life's challenges by reducing the negative effects of stress on the body.

HOLY BASIL (TULSI): AN ADAPTABLE HERB

Tulsi, also known as holy basil, is highly valued in ancient Ayurvedic medicine and is known for its adaptogenic properties. By regulating the release of stress hormones, holy basil functions as an adaptogenic plant, assisting the body in responding to external stressors. The term "elixir of life" is frequently used to describe it because of its all-encompassing advantages for mental, emotional, and physical health. Holy basil is well known for its ability to relax the nervous system and lessen tension and anxiety. Its immune-supporting qualities are part of its adaptogenic qualities, offering a whole strategy for preserving health under pressure. Furthermore, holy basil has a spiritual component to its use because it is revered as a sacred herb in Hinduism.

Including Holy Basil in a wellness regimen can help support a resilient and well-rounded approach to stress reduction.

Three exceptional adaptogenic herbs that provide all-encompassing methods of stress management are ashwagandha, Rhodiola Rosea, and holy basil. Every herb has special qualities that support the body's capacity to adjust and deal with stressors, fostering equilibrium and overall well-being. These adaptogens, when taken singly or in combination, may strengthen the body's resistance to weariness and promote serenity when confronted with obstacles in life. In the quest for optimum health, accepting the conventional understanding of these herbs creates opportunities for all-natural stress-reduction techniques.

CHAPTER SIX

TEAS AND INFUSIONS THAT PROMOTE SLEEP

TEA WITH LAVENDER: A AROMATIC SLEEP AID

Notable for its calming qualities, lavender tea is a fragrant and peaceful sleep aid. This herbal tea, which comes from the lavender plant, has been prized for generations because of its calming and sedative properties. Lavender is a great option for individuals looking for a quiet transitional scent before bed because it has a relaxing influence on the nervous system.

A good night's sleep can be achieved by reducing stress and anxiety through the use of lavender tea, which is made from the dried flowers of the lavender plant. Incorporating lavender tea into one's nighttime routine can be a nice addition, as it provides a scented solution for restful sleep in addition to a pleasant flavor.

TEA WITH PEPPERMINT: RELAXING THE NERVOUS SYSTEM

With its fresh flavor and energizing aroma, peppermint tea is a useful tool for relaxing the nervous system. In addition to tasting nice, peppermint tea has menthol, a substance with muscle-relaxing qualities. This makes it very useful for relieving stress and fostering serenity. Peppermint tea's menthol functions as a natural muscle relaxant, promoting mental and physical relaxation. Furthermore, drinking warm peppermint tea can be a reassuring habit in and of itself, sending a message to the body that it's time to relax. Peppermint tea helps to create a tranquil state that is ideal for a restful night's sleep by reducing tension and relaxing muscles.

INFUSION OF LEMON VERBENA: CALM IN A CUP

The scented lemon verbena plant's leaves are used to make lemon verbena infusion, which provides a pleasant and calming experience that may aid in relaxation. Lemon verbena's zesty and herbal notes combine to make a refreshing infusion that is not only pleasant to the taste buds but may also help induce sleep. An infusion of lemon verbena, which is high in antioxidants, has long been used to reduce stress and encourage calmness. The water is made into a mild and fragrant elixir by allowing the flavors and essential oils to seep into it during the infusion process. Drinking an infusion of lemon verbena before bed can be a sensory treat that promotes relaxation and creates the ideal environment for a restful night's sleep.

MAKING HERBAL SLEEP BLENDS: CREATING HERBAL INSOMNIA BLENDS

One satisfying and useful method for treating insomnia and encouraging sound sleep is to make a customized herbal sleep blend. The secret is to choose herbs that work well together and have relaxing qualities. Start by thinking about what you personally like because the blend's flavor and aroma can improve the whole experience. Herbs including chamomile, lavender, valerian, passionflower, and lemon balm are frequently used in sleep mixtures. Try out various combinations to determine which one suits you the best.

COMPREHENDING HERBAL SYNERGIES

Comprehending the inter-herbal interactions is essential when creating an herbal sleep combination. Synergy is the term used to describe how herbs work together to improve their combined benefits. For instance, chamomile and lavender are well known for their relaxing qualities, and when used together, they could have a stronger calming impact than when taken alone. Another combination that frequently complements one another is valerian and passionflower. You can customize your herbal combination to target particular symptoms of insomnia, including anxiety or trouble falling asleep, by investigating these synergies.

Advice for Preparing Herbal Infusions and Tinctures That Work: The way your herbal mix is made greatly influences how well it works. Herbal tinctures and infusions are two well-liked ways to draw out the healthful ingredients from herbs. Herbal infusions are made by steeping herbs in hot water for a predetermined amount of time, which allows the water to absorb the medicinal qualities of the herbs. Herbs are soaked in alcohol or another solvent to make concentrated liquid extracts for tinctures. To get the best extraction for your blend, try varying the ratios and steeping times.

For a more concentrated flavor, think about using dried herbs when creating infusions. Depending on your preferred level of infusion strength and personal taste, adjust the amount of herbs used. However, as tinctures can take several weeks to achieve their maximum strength, using them calls for patience. Throughout this time, shake the tincture frequently to guarantee complete extraction.

Be mindful of the quality of your herbs; adding fresh, organic herbs to your blend will increase its power. To keep your herbal compositions effective and fresh, proper storage is also necessary. Store them out of direct sunlight and dampness in a cold, dark place.

Creating your herbal sleep blend requires careful consideration of the plants you use, knowledge of their interactions, and proficiency in the art of creating potent tinctures and infusions. Accepting the holistic approach of herbal medicines allows you to design a customized, all-natural plan to relieve insomnia and encourage sound sleep.

CHAPTER SEVEN

LIFESTYLE AND PROPER SLEEP PRACTICES

THE FUNCTION OF DIET IN SLEEP

A vital component of keeping a balanced and healthful lifestyle is understanding the role that nutrition plays in sleep. Our sleep quality can be greatly impacted by the things we eat. It is critical to pay attention to the things we eat and when we eat them, especially in the hours before bed. Eating large or rich meals right before bed can cause indigestion and discomfort, which can throw off your sleep schedule. However, eating foods high in compounds that promote sleep, such as tryptophan, which is present in dairy, nuts, and turkey, can help you get a better night's rest.

CREATING A REGULAR SLEEP SCHEDULE

Another essential component of excellent sleep hygiene is creating a regular sleep pattern. Our bodies are routine creatures, and maintaining a regular sleep schedule aids in regulating the body's internal clock. Maintaining a consistent sleep and wake time every day, including on weekends, aids in regulating the body's circadian rhythm. The body's internal cues are reinforced by this consistency, which facilitates regular sleep and wakefulness cycles. A disturbed circadian rhythm may result from irregular sleep habits, which may make it difficult to fall asleep or have a good night's sleep.

ESTABLISHING A CALM NIGHTTIME SCHEDULE

Establishing a calming nighttime routine is an effective way to tell the body when it's time to wind down and get ready for sleep. Before going to bed, taking part in relaxing activities can assist in removing the tension of the day from the mind. This could involve things like reading a book, doing yoga or moderate stretches, or just relaxing with some music on. It's important to steer clear of stimulating activities during the sleep ritual, such as watching intense movies or working on work-related duties. The intention is to establish a calm and relaxing atmosphere that facilitates relaxation and eases the body and mind into a restful condition.

It's critical to understand the interconnectedness of several aspects, such as diet, sleep schedule, and bedtime routine, in addition to their separate contributions to the promotion of overall sleep hygiene. For example, a balanced diet takes into account the time of meals about the sleep schedule in addition to including foods that promote sleep. Similar to how a regular sleep schedule enhances a nighttime ritual, it offers an organized framework for unwinding activities.

In the end, a holistic approach to sleep hygiene and lifestyle calls for deliberates decisions in a range of spheres of daily living. Maintaining a healthy diet, sleep schedule, and nighttime habits all work together to create an atmosphere that promotes healthy sleep and overall vigor.

CHAPTER EIGHT

BLENDING HERBAL TREATMENTS WITH ALTERNATIVE THERAPIES

COMBINING COGNITIVE BEHAVIORAL THERAPY AND HERBAL MEDICINE FOR INSOMNIA (CBT-I)

Herbal medicine and Cognitive Behavioral Therapy for Insomnia (CBT-I) together offer a comprehensive strategy for treating sleep disorders. To enhance the quality of sleep, CBT-I is a well-researched therapy strategy that focuses on changing attitudes and behaviors linked to sleep.

Combined with herbal medicine, which frequently uses relaxing herbs like lavender, chamomile, and valerian, the synergistic benefits can increase the treatment's overall efficacy. These herbs are well-known for their calming qualities, which encourage rest and may lessen the tension or worry that fuels insomnia. Herbal medicines are used in CBT-I to address both the psychological and physiological aspects of insomnia, resulting in a more holistic and well-rounded approach to sleep therapy.

Yoga and Meditation for Better Sleep: As people look for all-natural, holistic ways to improve the quality of their sleep, incorporating yoga and meditation activities into sleep management regimens is becoming more and more common. Both yoga and meditation have their roots in age-old practices that emphasize the mind-body connection, and they can be very beneficial for treating sleep issues.

Yoga helps the body get ready for sleep by promoting physical relaxation and releasing tension through its meditative movements and gentle stretching. Contrarily, meditation promotes mental calmness and reduces tension and anxiety, which can exacerbate sleeplessness. These techniques work in harmony to address the complex nature of sleep disruptions when they are combined. Herbal treatments that encourage relaxation and stress reduction, including ashwagandha or passionflower, might further enhance these techniques.

THE COMBINATION OF HERBAL MEDICINES AND RELAXATION METHODS

Herbal medicines and relaxation practices work in concert to promote general well-being and lessen the negative effects of stress on the body and mind. Herbal treatments, which are frequently made from herbs like rhodiola or holy basil that have adaptogenic qualities, can assist the body in adjusting to stressors and act as a natural defense against the damaging effects of long-term stress.

The relaxing and centering benefits are enhanced when paired with other relaxation techniques such as progressive muscle relaxation, guided visualization, or deep breathing. The herbs provide supporting properties that improve the body's capacity for relaxation. This mix promotes a balanced and healthful response to life's obstacles by addressing both the short-term symptoms of stress and long-term resilience.

A holistic approach to well-being that acknowledges the connection between mental and physical health in the pursuit of optimal life is shown in the integration of herbal treatments with relaxation techniques.

CHAPTER NINE

SAFETY AND PRECAUTIONS

SPEAKING WITH A MEDICAL PROFESSIONAL

The fundamental idea of consulting with a healthcare practitioner is the first step towards guaranteeing safety and well-being in healthcare operations. Before beginning any new health-related initiative, especially one that requires medicine or therapy, people should always seek the advice and knowledge of a certified medical professional. Understanding unique health situations, possible hazards, and the appropriateness of particular interventions all depend on this consultation.

Healthcare practitioners are equipped with the requisite knowledge to assess a patient's medical background, current health issues, and any risk factors that could impact the efficacy and safety of a given treatment plan. Healthcare professionals can provide individualized recommendations by taking into account lifestyle choices, allergies, and pre-existing medical disorders.

Furthermore, consultation is a continuous process rather than a one-time occurrence that enables recommendations to be modified in response to a person's reaction to a specific intervention. It creates an essential avenue of communication via which people may express their worries, experiences, and any changes in their health that they may have noticed. Encouraging continuous communication is essential to maximizing the effectiveness and safety of medical decisions.

POSSIBLE DRUG INTERACTIONS

One of the most important aspects of making sure healthcare procedures are safe is being aware of and taking steps to mitigate any potential drug interactions. Many people may receive many prescriptions for drugs or supplements at the same time, and the interactions between these compounds can have a significant impact on overall health. Unintended consequences may arise from interactions involving changes in medication metabolism, absorption, distribution, or excretion.

Medical practitioners are essential in spotting any drug interactions by going over a patient's prescription history in detail. This covers over-the-counter, prescription, and dietary supplements. Dietary practices are also taken into account because some meals and beverages can interfere with drugs.

Open communication about all substances taken, including herbal treatments and alternative therapies, is essential between patients and healthcare practitioners. Because of this transparency, medical practitioners can make well-informed judgments regarding pharmaceutical regimens, dosage adjustments, and, if needed, the selection of alternative treatments.

DOSAGE RECOMMENDATIONS AND OVERSIGHT

Two essential components of ensuring patient safety during medical procedures are following recommended dosage guidelines and doing routine monitoring. Usually, dosages are recommended by each person's unique health profile, which includes things like age, weight, and general state of health. When dosages are not followed exactly, there may be negative side effects, decreased effectiveness, or even poisoning.

Specific dose instructions are given by medical professionals, and it is the responsibility of individuals to adhere to these instructions strictly. This entails following the frequency recommendations and refraining from self-adjusting dosages without seeing a physician. People should also be on the lookout for any possible adverse effects and notify their healthcare professionals right away if they have any strange symptoms.

A crucial component of healthcare interventions is monitoring, which enables medical personnel to evaluate the therapies' continuing effects and make any required modifications. This could be routine physical examinations, lab work, or other diagnostic procedures to assess the efficacy of treatments and spot any new problems.

A thorough approach to medication safety in healthcare entails speaking with medical experts, being aware of possible drug interactions, and closely following dosage recommendations with frequent monitoring. Together, these components optimize health outcomes while lowering risks and guaranteeing the welfare of patients receiving medical interventions.

Made in United States
Orlando, FL
03 June 2025

61814537R00026